The Future of Infrastructure Management
Exploring Cloud Computing for Students

Alice

Copyright © [2023]

Author: Alice

Title: The Future of Infrastructure Management Exploring Cloud Computing for Students

This book is a product of [Publisher's Alice]

ISBN:

TABLE OF CONTENTS

Chapter 5: Security and Privacy in Cloud Computing   55

Chapter 6: Future Trends and Emerging Technologies in Cloud Computing   67

Chapter 7: Best Practices for Students in Cloud Computing and Infrastructure Management   73

Chapter 8: Case Studies and Real-World Examples 81

Chapter 9: Conclusion and Future Outlook 87

Chapter 1: Introduction to Cloud Computing and Infrastructure Management

The Evolution of Infrastructure Management

In today's rapidly advancing technological landscape, infrastructure management has undergone a significant evolution. This subchapter will delve into the transformative journey of infrastructure management and highlight the pivotal role that cloud computing has played in this process. Aimed at students in the field of software engineering, this chapter will provide a comprehensive overview of the evolution of infrastructure management, equipping them with a deeper understanding of the subject.

Traditional infrastructure management involved the physical setup and maintenance of hardware and software systems within an organization. This approach was time-consuming, costly, and often resulted in limited scalability. However, with the advent of cloud computing, a paradigm shift occurred, revolutionizing the way infrastructure was managed.

Cloud computing introduced a new model where infrastructure resources, such as servers, storage, and networking, could be provisioned and managed remotely via the internet. This eliminated the need for physical infrastructure and allowed businesses to scale their operations quickly and efficiently. Students in the field of software engineering must grasp the significance of this shift and familiarize themselves with the underlying concepts and technologies.

The evolution of infrastructure management has given rise to various cloud computing models, such as Infrastructure as a Service (IaaS), Platform as a Service (PaaS), and Software as a Service (SaaS). Each of these models offers distinct advantages and caters to different needs. It is crucial for students to comprehend the differences between these models and understand how they fit into the broader infrastructure management landscape.

Furthermore, the subchapter will explore the benefits and challenges associated with cloud-based infrastructure management. While the cloud offers numerous advantages, including cost savings, flexibility, and enhanced security, it also presents challenges such as data privacy concerns and reliance on third-party service providers. Students must be aware of these factors and learn how to navigate them effectively.

To conclude, the evolution of infrastructure management has been shaped by cloud computing, opening up new possibilities for businesses and organizations. By understanding the journey from traditional infrastructure management to the cloud-based approach, students in the field of software engineering can position themselves as leaders in this rapidly evolving domain. This subchapter will serve as a foundation for their knowledge acquisition, enabling them to harness the power of cloud computing in their future careers.

The Importance of Cloud Computing in Infrastructure Management

In today's digital age, where technology is advancing at an unprecedented pace, it is crucial for students pursuing software engineering to understand the significance of cloud computing in infrastructure management. Cloud computing has emerged as a game-changer in the field, revolutionizing the way software and applications are developed, deployed, and managed.

Cloud computing refers to the delivery of computing resources, including servers, storage, databases, networking, and software, over the internet. It allows users to access these resources on-demand, without the need for physical infrastructure. This paradigm shift has brought about numerous benefits that are particularly relevant to the field of software engineering.

One of the key advantages of cloud computing in infrastructure management is scalability. Traditional infrastructure often requires significant upfront investment to accommodate future growth. However, with cloud computing, students can easily scale their resources up or down based on demand. This flexibility allows software engineers to develop and test applications without worrying about infrastructure limitations, thereby enhancing productivity and reducing costs.

Another crucial aspect is the increased reliability and availability offered by cloud computing. Cloud service providers typically have redundant data centers spread across different geographical locations, ensuring that applications and data remain accessible even in the event of hardware failures or natural disasters. This high level of reliability is essential for software engineers, as it minimizes downtime and ensures seamless service delivery to end-users.

Furthermore, cloud computing enables students to experiment with new technologies and frameworks without investing in expensive hardware or software licenses. They can leverage the vast array of cloud-based development tools, platforms, and services to build innovative applications, gain hands-on experience, and stay updated with the latest industry trends. This access to cutting-edge technologies empowers students to enhance their skills and become proficient software engineers.

Moreover, cloud computing offers improved collaboration and teamwork opportunities. Students can work on projects together, accessing and editing files simultaneously from different locations. This enhances communication, fosters creativity, and prepares them for the collaborative nature of the software engineering industry.

In conclusion, cloud computing plays a pivotal role in infrastructure management for software engineering students. Its scalability, reliability, cost-effectiveness, access to advanced technologies, and enhanced collaboration capabilities make it an essential tool for students to excel in their field. By understanding the importance of cloud computing, students can stay ahead of the curve and embrace the future of infrastructure management.

Benefits and Challenges of Cloud Computing for Students

In today's digital age, cloud computing has emerged as a revolutionary technology that is transforming the way we store, access, and manage data. For students, particularly those studying software engineering, cloud computing offers a plethora of benefits but also comes with its fair share of challenges. This subchapter will explore the advantages and drawbacks of cloud computing specifically tailored to the needs of students in the field of software engineering.

One of the key benefits of cloud computing for students is its accessibility. With cloud-based services, students can access their study materials, projects, and software tools from anywhere, at any time, using any device with an internet connection. Gone are the days of carrying around bulky laptops or USB drives filled with important files. Cloud computing enables students to work on assignments collaboratively, allowing for seamless integration and real-time collaboration with their peers.

Another advantage of cloud computing is its cost-effectiveness. As students, budget constraints are a common concern. By utilizing cloud services, students can save on hardware and software expenses, as cloud providers handle the infrastructure and maintenance costs. Moreover, cloud computing allows for easy scalability, meaning students can easily upgrade or downgrade their storage and computing resources as per their needs, without incurring additional expenses.

Cloud computing also offers enhanced security for students. Cloud-based platforms typically have robust security measures in place, including encryption, authentication, and data backup. This ensures that students' valuable work and personal information are protected from potential data loss or security breaches.

However, along with its benefits, cloud computing also poses certain challenges. One of the main concerns is the issue of data privacy. Students must be cautious about the information they store on the cloud and ensure they are aware of the privacy policies of the cloud service provider they choose. It is crucial to understand where their data is being stored and who has access to it.

Another challenge is the reliance on internet connectivity. Since cloud computing heavily relies on internet access, students may face difficulties if they encounter slow or unreliable internet connections. This can disrupt their work, especially when dealing with large files or running resource-intensive software.

In conclusion, cloud computing offers numerous advantages for students in the field of software engineering. Its accessibility, cost-effectiveness, and enhanced security make it an invaluable tool in their academic journey. However, students must also be aware of the challenges, such as data privacy concerns and reliance on internet connectivity. By understanding these aspects, students can harness the power of cloud computing to streamline their studies and enhance their learning experience.

Chapter 2: Fundamentals of Cloud Computing

Understanding Cloud Computing Concepts

Cloud computing has emerged as a revolutionary technology that has transformed the way we store, process, and access data. In this subchapter, we will delve into the fundamental concepts of cloud computing, exploring its various components and their significance in the field of software engineering.

At its core, cloud computing refers to the delivery of computing services over the internet, allowing users to access and utilize a vast network of remote servers. This infrastructure provides a range of services, including storage, processing power, and software applications, without the need for local servers or personal computing devices. Understanding the key concepts behind cloud computing is essential for software engineering students, as it enables them to leverage the full potential of this technology in their projects and future careers.

One of the fundamental concepts in cloud computing is virtualization. It involves creating virtual instances of computing resources, such as servers or storage devices, enabling multiple users to share the same physical infrastructure. By virtualizing resources, cloud service providers can maximize their efficiency and utilization, while users can easily scale their computing resources based on their needs.

Another crucial concept is scalability. Cloud computing allows for on-demand resource allocation, meaning that users can easily scale up or down their computing resources in response to workload fluctuations. This flexibility is particularly valuable for software engineers, as it allows them to handle varying demands for their applications without the need for substantial investments in hardware or infrastructure.

Furthermore, the concept of elasticity is closely related to scalability. Elasticity refers to the ability of a cloud system to automatically provision and de-provision resources based on current demand. This dynamic allocation ensures optimal resource utilization and cost efficiency, making cloud computing an attractive option for software engineering projects with fluctuating workloads.

In addition to these concepts, security is of paramount importance in cloud computing. Students must understand the various security measures and protocols employed by cloud service providers to protect data and ensure privacy. These measures include encryption, access control, and regular security audits, which collectively contribute to a secure cloud computing environment.

By comprehending these core concepts of cloud computing, software engineering students can effectively utilize the cloud infrastructure in their projects, improve scalability and efficiency, and ensure the security of their applications and data. As cloud computing continues to revolutionize the field of infrastructure management, students must stay abreast of the latest developments and explore the potential of this technology for their future careers.

Definition and Characteristics of Cloud Computing

Cloud computing has emerged as a revolutionary technology that has greatly influenced the field of software engineering. In this subchapter, we will provide an overview of cloud computing, its definition, and the key characteristics that make it an essential part of infrastructure management in the modern era.

Cloud computing can be defined as the delivery of computing services, including storage, processing power, and software applications, over the internet on-demand. Unlike traditional computing models, where software and hardware resources are installed locally on individual computers, cloud computing enables users to access these resources remotely through the internet. This concept has transformed the way software engineers design, develop, and deploy applications.

One of the key characteristics of cloud computing is scalability. With cloud services, software engineers can easily scale up or down their computing resources based on demand without the need for physical infrastructure modifications. This flexibility allows for efficient resource allocation, cost optimization, and the ability to handle sudden spikes in user traffic without disruptions.

Another characteristic of cloud computing is its virtualization capabilities. Virtualization enables the creation of multiple virtual machines (VMs) or containers on a single physical server, allowing for better utilization of computing resources. Software engineers can deploy applications on these virtual environments, ensuring efficient use of hardware and reducing costs associated with maintaining physical servers.

Cloud computing also offers a pay-as-you-go pricing model, which means that software engineers only pay for the resources they consume. This eliminates the need for large upfront investments in hardware and software licenses, making cloud computing accessible to students and small-scale software engineering projects.

Furthermore, cloud computing provides enhanced reliability and availability. Cloud service providers offer robust infrastructure with redundant systems, ensuring that applications remain accessible even in the event of hardware failures. Software engineers can take advantage of this feature to build highly available and fault-tolerant applications without investing in complex infrastructure setups.

In conclusion, cloud computing is a transformative technology that has revolutionized the field of software engineering. Its definition and characteristics, including scalability, virtualization, pay-as-you-go pricing, and enhanced reliability, make it an indispensable tool for students and professionals alike. Understanding and harnessing the power of cloud computing can significantly enhance the efficiency and effectiveness of infrastructure management in the software engineering domain.

Types of Cloud Services (IaaS, PaaS, SaaS)

In today's digital era, cloud computing has revolutionized the way software engineering is conducted. This chapter explores the various types of cloud services that are changing the landscape of infrastructure management. As students pursuing software engineering, it is crucial to understand these services and their implications on the future of our field.

Infrastructure as a Service (IaaS) is the first type of cloud service we will explore. With IaaS, students have access to virtualized computing resources over the internet. This means that instead of investing in physical servers and networking equipment, students can leverage the cloud to provision and manage these resources remotely. IaaS provides a flexible and scalable infrastructure, allowing students to focus on their software development without worrying about the underlying hardware.

Platform as a Service (PaaS) is the next type of cloud service that software engineering students should be familiar with. PaaS offers a complete development and deployment environment, enabling students to build, test, and deploy their applications without worrying about the underlying infrastructure. PaaS platforms provide a wide range of services, including development frameworks, databases, and application servers. By leveraging PaaS, students can streamline their development process and focus on writing code instead of managing infrastructure.

Software as a Service (SaaS) is a cloud service that has gained immense popularity in recent years. SaaS allows students to access software applications over the internet, without the need for installation or maintenance. This means that students can use SaaS platforms for various purposes, such as collaboration, project management, or data analysis. SaaS eliminates the need for students to invest in expensive software licenses and hardware, providing a cost-effective solution for their software engineering needs.

Understanding the different types of cloud services is essential for students pursuing software engineering. These services offer numerous benefits, such as scalability, flexibility, and cost-effectiveness. By leveraging IaaS, PaaS, and SaaS, students can focus on their software development projects without being burdened by the complexities of infrastructure management.

In conclusion, cloud computing has transformed the way software engineering is conducted, and it is crucial for students in this field to understand the various types of cloud services available. IaaS, PaaS, and SaaS offer students the opportunity to leverage scalable infrastructure, complete development environments, and software applications over the internet. By embracing these cloud services, students can enhance their software engineering skills and adapt to the evolving technology landscape.

Cloud Service Providers

Cloud computing has revolutionized the way we store, access, and manage data. As a software engineering student, it is crucial to understand the concept of cloud service providers and their role in enabling cloud computing. In this subchapter, we will delve into the world of cloud service providers and explore their significance in the field of software engineering.

Cloud service providers are companies that offer various cloud-based services to individuals and organizations. These services include infrastructure as a service (IaaS), platform as a service (PaaS), and software as a service (SaaS). The primary goal of cloud service providers is to provide scalable, reliable, and cost-effective solutions to users.

One of the most well-known cloud service providers is Amazon Web Services (AWS). AWS offers a wide range of services, including virtual servers, databases, storage, and developer tools. It provides an easily scalable infrastructure, allowing software engineers to build, deploy, and manage applications efficiently.

Another popular cloud service provider is Microsoft Azure. Azure offers a comprehensive suite of cloud services, including virtual machines, databases, AI, and analytics tools. With Azure, software engineers can develop and deploy applications seamlessly, taking advantage of its extensive ecosystem.

Google Cloud Platform (GCP) is another significant player in the cloud service provider market. GCP offers a plethora of services, including compute, storage, machine learning, and data analytics. It provides an excellent platform for software engineers to build, test, and deploy applications with ease.

Why should software engineering students pay attention to cloud service providers? Firstly, cloud service providers offer a vast array of resources and tools that can enhance the development process. By utilizing these services, software engineers can focus more on coding and innovation rather than worrying about the underlying infrastructure.

Secondly, cloud service providers offer cost-effective solutions. As a student, budget constraints are common, and building and maintaining physical infrastructure can be expensive. Cloud service providers eliminate the need for significant upfront investments by providing scalable and pay-as-you-go pricing models.

Furthermore, cloud service providers offer global accessibility and scalability. With the cloud, software engineers can deploy applications worldwide, making them accessible to users from different regions. Additionally, the scalability of cloud service providers allows applications to handle varying amounts of traffic without the need for manual intervention.

In conclusion, cloud service providers play a vital role in the field of software engineering. They offer a wide range of services, resources, and tools that enhance the development process. As a software engineering student, understanding and utilizing cloud service providers' capabilities can greatly benefit your career, enabling you to build innovative applications efficiently and cost-effectively.

Leading Cloud Service Providers

When it comes to cloud computing, there are several leading service providers that offer a range of solutions and services to meet the needs of businesses and individuals alike. These providers have established themselves as industry leaders in terms of reliability, scalability, security, and performance. In this subchapter, we will explore some of the leading cloud service providers and discuss their offerings.

1. Amazon Web Services (AWS): AWS is widely regarded as the pioneer and market leader in cloud computing services. It offers a comprehensive suite of services, including computing power, storage, databases, analytics, and machine learning. AWS provides a highly flexible and scalable infrastructure that enables businesses to deploy applications and services quickly and efficiently.

2. Microsoft Azure: Azure is a cloud computing platform offered by Microsoft. It provides a wide range of services, including virtual machines, databases, storage, and AI capabilities. Azure is known for its strong integration with Microsoft products and services, making it an attractive choice for businesses already using Microsoft technologies.

3. Google Cloud Platform (GCP): GCP is Google's cloud computing service that offers infrastructure and platform services for running applications. It provides a robust set of tools and services for data storage, analytics, machine learning, and application development. GCP is known for its strong emphasis on data analytics and machine learning capabilities.

4. IBM Cloud: IBM Cloud is a comprehensive cloud computing platform that combines Infrastructure as a Service (IaaS), Platform as a

Service (PaaS), and Software as a Service (SaaS) offerings. It provides a range of services, including compute power, storage, networking, and AI capabilities. IBM Cloud is recognized for its enterprise-grade security and compliance features.

5. Oracle Cloud: Oracle Cloud is a cloud computing service offered by Oracle Corporation. It provides a range of services, including infrastructure, databases, analytics, and AI capabilities. Oracle Cloud is known for its strong focus on enterprise applications and its ability to seamlessly integrate with existing Oracle databases and applications.

These leading cloud service providers offer a wealth of resources and services that are essential for software engineering students. By leveraging these platforms, students can gain hands-on experience in developing and deploying applications in a cloud environment. Furthermore, these providers offer various certification programs that can enhance students' credentials and increase their employability in the software engineering field.

In conclusion, the leading cloud service providers, such as AWS, Azure, GCP, IBM Cloud, and Oracle Cloud, offer a wide range of services and tools that are crucial for software engineering students. By familiarizing themselves with these platforms, students can gain practical experience and develop the necessary skills to excel in the field of cloud computing.

Comparison of Cloud Service Providers for Students

As a student studying software engineering, it is crucial to understand the various cloud service providers available and their offerings. Cloud computing has revolutionized the way we store, access, and process data, making it an indispensable tool for students in today's digital age. This subchapter aims to provide an overview and comparison of popular cloud service providers, helping students make informed decisions when choosing the right provider for their needs.

1. Amazon Web Services (AWS): AWS is the leading cloud service provider, offering a wide range of services including storage, compute power, databases, and developer tools. With its extensive ecosystem, AWS provides students with the flexibility to experiment, develop, and deploy applications seamlessly.

2. Microsoft Azure: Azure is another prominent player in the cloud computing market. It offers a comprehensive suite of services, including virtual machines, storage, and AI capabilities. As a student, Azure provides access to a vast array of tools and resources, enabling you to build and deploy applications effortlessly.

3. Google Cloud Platform (GCP): GCP is Google's cloud service platform that provides a scalable and reliable infrastructure for students. With its strong focus on machine learning and data analytics, GCP offers unique opportunities for those interested in these areas of software engineering. GCP also provides robust networking capabilities and a user-friendly interface.

4. IBM Cloud: IBM Cloud is known for its enterprise-grade infrastructure and services. As a student, you can benefit from IBM's extensive offerings, including AI, blockchain, and IoT services. IBM

Cloud also provides a range of tools and resources specifically designed for software engineering students.

5. Oracle Cloud: Oracle Cloud offers a comprehensive suite of infrastructure, platform, and software services. With its focus on enterprise applications and database management systems, Oracle Cloud provides students with the opportunity to gain hands-on experience in these areas.

When comparing these cloud service providers, factors such as cost, ease of use, availability of resources, and scalability should be considered. Most providers offer free tiers or credits for students, allowing you to explore and experiment without incurring significant costs.

Ultimately, the choice of cloud service provider depends on your specific requirements and learning goals. It is recommended to explore the documentation, tutorials, and support offered by each provider to evaluate which one aligns best with your needs.

By understanding the offerings of different cloud service providers, students can harness the power of cloud computing to enhance their software engineering skills, develop innovative applications, and prepare themselves for the future of infrastructure management.

Chapter 3: Infrastructure Management in Cloud Computing

Infrastructure as a Service (IaaS)

In the constantly evolving world of technology, cloud computing has emerged as a game-changer, and Infrastructure as a Service (IaaS) is at the forefront of this revolution. As students pursuing a career in software engineering, it is crucial to understand the concept of IaaS and its significance in today's digital landscape.

IaaS refers to a cloud computing model where virtualized infrastructure resources are provided to users over the internet. Instead of investing in physical infrastructure such as servers, storage, and networking equipment, organizations can now leverage IaaS to access and manage their IT infrastructure remotely. This model offers several advantages, making it highly appealing to businesses of all sizes.

One of the primary benefits of IaaS is its scalability. With traditional infrastructure, scaling up or down requires significant time and resources. However, with IaaS, students and organizations can easily adjust their resource allocation based on their needs. This flexibility allows software engineers to focus on developing and deploying applications without worrying about infrastructure limitations.

Moreover, IaaS eliminates the need for upfront capital investment, making it a cost-effective solution. Students can experiment with different infrastructure configurations without the burden of purchasing expensive hardware. This empowers them to learn and innovate without financial constraints, ultimately enhancing their skills in software engineering.

Additionally, IaaS offers a higher level of reliability and security compared to on-premises infrastructure. Cloud service providers ensure that data is stored securely and backups are performed regularly. This not only minimizes the risk of data loss but also provides students with peace of mind knowing that their work is protected.

By leveraging IaaS, software engineering students can also gain exposure to cutting-edge technologies. Cloud service providers constantly update their infrastructure to incorporate the latest advancements, allowing students to work with state-of-the-art tools and services. This exposure to modern technology prepares them for the dynamic and competitive software engineering industry.

In conclusion, Infrastructure as a Service (IaaS) is a revolutionary concept in cloud computing that offers numerous benefits to software engineering students. Its scalability, cost-effectiveness, reliability, and access to advanced technologies make it an essential component of the future of infrastructure management. By embracing IaaS, students can enhance their skills, innovate without financial constraints, and stay ahead in the ever-evolving field of software engineering.

Virtualization in IaaS

In recent years, cloud computing has gained significant momentum and has become an integral part of the technology landscape. It has revolutionized the way businesses manage their infrastructure by providing on-demand access to resources and services over the internet. One of the key components of cloud computing is Infrastructure as a Service (IaaS), which offers virtualized computing resources to users.

Virtualization is a fundamental concept in IaaS that enables the efficient utilization of physical hardware resources. It allows multiple virtual machines (VMs) to run on a single physical server, thereby maximizing the utilization and reducing costs. This technology has transformed the way software engineers approach infrastructure management.

Virtualization in IaaS provides several benefits to software engineering students and professionals. Firstly, it allows them to create and manage multiple VMs with different operating systems and configurations on a single physical server. This capability is incredibly useful for software development and testing purposes, as it enables the creation of isolated environments to test various software applications.

Furthermore, virtualization simplifies the process of deploying and scaling applications. With IaaS, students can easily provision new VM instances or scale up existing ones to meet the demands of their software projects. This flexibility ensures that the infrastructure can adapt to changing requirements without the need for physical hardware changes.

Another advantage of virtualization in IaaS is the ability to abstract the underlying hardware from software applications. This abstraction layer allows software engineers to focus solely on developing and managing their applications, without having to worry about the underlying infrastructure. It promotes faster development cycles and reduces the time spent on infrastructure management tasks.

Moreover, virtualization in IaaS enhances the resilience and availability of software applications. By running multiple VMs on different physical servers, it provides built-in redundancy and fault tolerance. In the event of a hardware failure, the affected VMs can be automatically migrated to other healthy servers, minimizing downtime and ensuring continuous service availability.

In conclusion, virtualization in IaaS is a game-changer for software engineering students. It empowers them to efficiently manage infrastructure resources, create isolated environments for software development, and simplify the deployment and scaling of applications. By leveraging the benefits of virtualization, students can focus more on their software projects and gain valuable experience in cloud computing, ultimately preparing them for the future of infrastructure management.

Scalability and Elasticity in IaaS

In the ever-evolving world of technology, the demand for scalable and elastic infrastructure has become paramount. This is particularly true for software engineering students who are at the forefront of developing and managing complex applications. In this subchapter, we will explore the concepts of scalability and elasticity in Infrastructure as a Service (IaaS) and how they are shaping the future of infrastructure management.

Scalability refers to the ability of a system to handle increasing workloads by adding or removing resources. In the context of IaaS, it means that students can easily scale up or down their infrastructure based on the demands of their applications. Whether it is a sudden surge in user traffic or the need for additional computing power, scalability allows students to meet these requirements without any hassle. IaaS providers offer flexible resource allocation and management tools, enabling software engineering students to scale their infrastructure seamlessly.

Elasticity, on the other hand, takes scalability to the next level by automatically adjusting resources based on real-time demand. This means that students no longer need to manually allocate or remove resources as the system can intelligently handle the fluctuations in workload. Elasticity ensures optimal resource utilization and cost-efficiency by dynamically provisioning or deprovisioning resources as needed. This is particularly beneficial for software engineering students who may experience varying levels of usage throughout the development and testing phases of their applications.

Implementing scalability and elasticity in IaaS offers several advantages for software engineering students. Firstly, it enables them to focus on application development rather than worrying about infrastructure management. By leveraging the scalability and elasticity features provided by IaaS providers, students can easily adapt to changing requirements and deliver high-performance applications.

Secondly, scalability and elasticity in IaaS facilitate cost optimization. With traditional infrastructure management, students often overprovision resources to handle occasional spikes in workload, resulting in unnecessary costs. However, with the ability to scale and adjust resources in real-time, students can optimize their infrastructure costs and only pay for what they actually use.

Lastly, scalability and elasticity in IaaS pave the way for innovation and experimentation. Students can rapidly prototype and test their applications without worrying about the limitations of their infrastructure. They can easily add or remove resources, test different configurations, and explore new technologies, all without any constraints. This fosters a culture of innovation and allows students to push the boundaries of software engineering.

In conclusion, scalability and elasticity in IaaS are transforming the way software engineering students manage infrastructure. By providing the ability to scale up or down resources and automatically adjust them based on demand, students can focus on application development, optimize costs, and foster innovation. Embracing these concepts will undoubtedly shape the future of infrastructure management in the field of software engineering.

Platform as a Service (PaaS)

In the ever-evolving world of software engineering, Platform as a Service (PaaS) has emerged as a game-changing concept that allows developers to focus more on their core competencies rather than worrying about infrastructure management. PaaS provides a complete development and deployment environment in the cloud, enabling software engineers to build, test, and deploy applications without the hassle of setting up and maintaining the underlying infrastructure.

PaaS offers a wide range of benefits for software engineering students looking to gain a competitive edge in the fast-paced technology industry. Firstly, it eliminates the need for high upfront capital investments in hardware and software, as the infrastructure is provided and managed by the PaaS provider. This allows students to experiment and prototype their ideas without financial constraints, fostering innovation and creativity.

Moreover, PaaS offers a streamlined development process by providing pre-configured development tools, libraries, and frameworks. This not only accelerates the development lifecycle but also ensures compatibility and reduces the chances of errors caused by inconsistent configurations. Students can focus on writing code and building applications, rather than spending time on mundane tasks like setting up databases or configuring servers.

Furthermore, PaaS facilitates collaboration among software engineering teams. With its centralized platform, multiple developers can work simultaneously on the same project, enhancing productivity and efficiency. PaaS also enables seamless integration with version control systems, allowing developers to track changes, collaborate on code, and ensure code quality through continuous integration and automated testing.

In addition to these benefits, PaaS provides scalability and flexibility, allowing applications to easily adapt to changing workloads and user demands. As students develop their skills in software engineering, they can leverage the scalability of PaaS to handle increasing traffic and user data without worrying about the underlying infrastructure.

Overall, PaaS is a game-changer for software engineering students, enabling them to focus on their core competencies, streamline development processes, foster collaboration, and scale applications seamlessly. By leveraging PaaS, students can gain practical experience in modern software development practices, preparing them for the dynamic and challenging world of cloud computing.

Development and Deployment in PaaS

In today's rapidly evolving technological landscape, the demand for efficient and scalable infrastructure management solutions has grown exponentially. Cloud computing has emerged as a game-changing technology that addresses these needs by providing a flexible and cost-effective platform for software development and deployment. This subchapter aims to explore the concept of Platform as a Service (PaaS) and its role in the development and deployment processes, especially for students and professionals in the field of Software Engineering.

PaaS offers a comprehensive suite of tools and services that enable developers to focus on building and deploying applications without the hassle of managing underlying infrastructure. It provides a ready-to-use platform with pre-configured runtime environments, development frameworks, and scalable databases, allowing developers to quickly iterate their code and deliver high-quality software solutions.

One key advantage of PaaS is its ability to streamline the development process. Developers can leverage the platform's integrated development environment (IDE) to write, test, and debug their code in a collaborative and efficient manner. PaaS also supports version control systems, making it easier to manage code revisions and collaborate with team members.

Furthermore, PaaS simplifies the deployment process by offering automated build and release mechanisms. Students can utilize continuous integration and continuous deployment (CI/CD) pipelines to automate the testing, building, and deployment of their applications, thereby reducing time-to-market and ensuring a seamless user experience.

Another crucial aspect of PaaS is its scalability and cost-effectiveness. Students can benefit from PaaS providers' ability to dynamically allocate resources based on application demand. This ensures optimal performance and cost efficiency, as resources are scaled up or down automatically. Moreover, PaaS eliminates the need for upfront infrastructure investments and reduces operational costs, making it an attractive option for students and startups with limited budgets.

However, students must consider certain factors when choosing a PaaS provider. They should evaluate the platform's compatibility with their preferred programming languages, frameworks, and databases. Additionally, security, data privacy, and vendor lock-in should be carefully assessed to mitigate potential risks.

In conclusion, PaaS is revolutionizing the way software is developed and deployed. Its simplicity, scalability, and cost-effectiveness make it an invaluable tool for students and professionals in the field of Software Engineering. By leveraging PaaS, students can focus on innovation and rapidly bring their ideas to market, ultimately shaping the future of infrastructure management.

Benefits and Limitations of PaaS for Students

As students in the field of software engineering, it is essential to understand the various tools and technologies that can enhance our learning and development. One such technology that has revolutionized the way we build and deploy applications is Platform as a Service (PaaS). In this subchapter, we will explore the benefits and limitations of PaaS for students, providing insights into how this cloud computing model can empower us in our academic pursuits.

Firstly, PaaS offers numerous benefits for students in software engineering. One of the major advantages is the ease of use and convenience it provides. With PaaS, students can access a preconfigured development environment with all the necessary tools and frameworks readily available. This eliminates the hassle of setting up a local development environment and allows us to focus on learning and coding rather than dealing with infrastructure complexities.

Furthermore, PaaS offers scalability and flexibility, allowing students to easily scale their applications based on demand. This is particularly useful when working on projects that may require additional resources or when collaborating with a team on a larger-scale project. PaaS platforms also provide seamless integration with other cloud services, enabling students to leverage various services such as databases, storage, and analytics without the need for extensive configuration.

Another significant benefit of PaaS for students is cost-effectiveness. Most PaaS providers offer a pay-as-you-go pricing model, allowing students to utilize the resources they need without the burden of heavy upfront costs. This makes it an attractive option for students who may have limited budgets.

However, it is important to acknowledge the limitations of PaaS as well. One of the main concerns is the potential lack of control over the underlying infrastructure. While PaaS abstracts the complexities of infrastructure management, it also means that students may have limited control over certain aspects of their applications. This can be a challenge for students who want to have full control and customization over their development environment.

Additionally, reliance on third-party providers for infrastructure and services can introduce potential security and privacy concerns. Students must be mindful of the data they store and the security measures implemented by the PaaS provider to ensure the confidentiality and integrity of their work.

In conclusion, PaaS offers numerous benefits for students in the field of software engineering. It simplifies the development process, provides scalability and flexibility, and offers cost-effectiveness. However, it is important to consider the limitations, such as the lack of control over infrastructure and potential security concerns. By understanding these benefits and limitations, students can make informed decisions about incorporating PaaS into their academic endeavors, ultimately enhancing their learning experiences in the ever-evolving world of cloud computing.

Software as a Service (SaaS)

In today's digital age, cloud computing has revolutionized the way software is delivered and consumed. One of the most popular cloud computing models is Software as a Service (SaaS). SaaS offers students and software engineering professionals a flexible and cost-effective solution for accessing and utilizing software applications.

SaaS eliminates the need for individuals to install and maintain software on their own computers or devices. Instead, the software is hosted and managed by a service provider, who delivers it over the internet. This means that students and software engineering professionals can access the software from any device with an internet connection, saving them the hassle of installation and updates.

One of the key advantages of SaaS is its scalability. Students can easily scale up or down their usage based on their needs, paying only for what they use. This makes it an ideal solution for software engineering projects that require varying levels of resources and collaboration.

SaaS also offers students the opportunity to work on cutting-edge software applications without the need for expensive hardware or extensive technical knowledge. With SaaS, they can simply log in to the software and start using its features and functionalities. This allows them to focus more on their projects and assignments, rather than spending time and effort on software installation and configuration.

Additionally, SaaS provides students with the ability to collaborate and share their work with their peers and instructors. They can easily grant access to others, allowing for real-time collaboration and feedback. This fosters a more interactive and engaging learning experience, as students can work together on projects and learn from each other's expertise.

From a software engineering perspective, SaaS offers numerous benefits. It allows software engineers to focus on developing and improving the core functionalities of the software, rather than worrying about its deployment and maintenance. SaaS providers take care of infrastructure management, security, and software updates, ensuring that the software is always up-to-date and reliable.

In conclusion, Software as a Service (SaaS) is a game-changer in the field of software engineering, offering students and professionals a cost-effective and flexible solution for accessing and utilizing software applications. With its scalability, ease of use, and collaboration features, SaaS empowers students to work on projects and assignments more efficiently, while allowing software engineers to focus on innovation and development. Embracing SaaS can greatly enhance the future of infrastructure management in the cloud computing era.

Common SaaS Applications for Students

In today's digital age, cloud computing has revolutionized the way we access and utilize software applications. Software as a Service (SaaS) has emerged as a popular model for delivering software applications over the internet, providing students with easy access to a wide range of tools and resources. This subchapter explores some of the common SaaS applications that are particularly beneficial for students in the field of software engineering.

1. Code Editors and IDEs: SaaS applications like Visual Studio Code, Eclipse Che, and Cloud9 provide students with powerful code editing and integrated development environments (IDEs) that can be accessed from any device with an internet connection. These tools offer features like real-time collaboration, syntax highlighting, and code completion, enhancing the coding experience for students.

2. Project Management Tools: Students working on software engineering projects can benefit from SaaS project management tools such as Trello, Asana, and Jira. These tools allow for efficient task management, collaboration, and tracking of project progress, enabling students to stay organized and meet project deadlines.

3. Version Control Systems: Git and GitHub are popular SaaS applications that facilitate version control and collaboration on code repositories. These tools enable students to track changes, manage code branches, and collaborate with others seamlessly, making it easier to work on group projects and contribute to open-source communities.

4. Testing and Debugging Tools: SaaS applications like Selenium and BrowserStack provide students with web testing and debugging

capabilities. These tools allow for automated testing across multiple browsers and operating systems, helping students ensure the quality and compatibility of their software applications.

5. Cloud Storage and Collaboration: SaaS applications like Google Drive, Dropbox, and OneDrive offer cloud storage solutions that allow students to store and share their files securely. These tools also enable real-time collaboration, allowing multiple students to work on documents, spreadsheets, and presentations simultaneously.

6. Learning Management Systems (LMS): SaaS-based LMS platforms like Canvas, Blackboard, and Moodle provide students with a centralized hub for accessing course materials, submitting assignments, participating in discussions, and tracking their progress. These platforms enhance the learning experience by providing a structured and interactive online learning environment.

By leveraging these SaaS applications, students in the field of software engineering can enhance their productivity, collaboration, and overall learning experience. The flexibility and accessibility offered by cloud-based software applications empower students to work on projects, collaborate with peers, and access resources from anywhere, at any time. Embracing these tools not only prepares students for the future of infrastructure management but also equips them with the skills and knowledge required to thrive in the digital age.

Security Considerations for SaaS in Education

In today's digital era, cloud computing has revolutionized the way we access and store data. One of its most widely adopted models is Software as a Service (SaaS), which is gaining significant popularity in the education sector. SaaS offers numerous benefits to educational institutions, such as cost-effectiveness, scalability, and easy accessibility. However, it is crucial to address the security considerations associated with SaaS in education to ensure the protection of sensitive student information and maintain a secure learning environment.

One of the primary security concerns when using SaaS in education is data privacy. Educational institutions handle vast amounts of sensitive student data, including personal information, academic records, and financial details. Therefore, it is essential to choose SaaS providers that prioritize data privacy and comply with relevant data protection regulations, such as the General Data Protection Regulation (GDPR). Students should be aware of the measures taken by their educational institutions and SaaS providers to secure their data, including encryption, access controls, and regular data backups.

Another critical aspect to consider is user authentication and access control. Educational SaaS platforms must implement robust authentication mechanisms to ensure that only authorized individuals can access sensitive data. Strong and unique passwords, multi-factor authentication, and role-based access control are some of the security measures that should be in place. Students should also be encouraged to follow best practices for password management, such as using complex passwords and avoiding sharing their login credentials.

Furthermore, educational institutions should regularly assess the security posture of their SaaS providers. This includes conducting thorough vendor assessments to evaluate their security practices, certifications, and incident response protocols. Students should have access to information regarding the security measures implemented by their SaaS providers, as well as any security incidents or breaches that may have occurred in the past.

Educational institutions should also educate their students on cybersecurity best practices. Students need to be aware of the potential risks associated with using SaaS platforms, such as phishing attacks, malware, and social engineering. They should be trained on how to identify and report suspicious activities, employ safe browsing habits, and use antivirus software to protect their devices.

In conclusion, while SaaS offers numerous benefits for educational institutions, it is essential to consider the security implications. Data privacy, user authentication, vendor assessments, and student awareness are all critical factors that should be addressed to ensure the secure adoption of SaaS in education. By understanding these security considerations and following best practices, students can make the most of cloud computing while minimizing the risks associated with it.

Chapter 4: Cloud Computing in Educational Institutions

Cloud Computing Adoption in Educational Institutions

In recent years, the adoption of cloud computing has become increasingly prevalent in educational institutions, revolutionizing the way students and educators interact with technology. This subchapter aims to provide students, particularly those studying software engineering, with insights into the benefits and challenges of cloud computing adoption in educational settings.

Cloud computing refers to the practice of using remote servers hosted on the internet to store, manage, and process data, rather than relying on local servers or personal computers. Educational institutions are increasingly leveraging cloud computing to enhance their infrastructure management and provide students with a more efficient learning experience.

One of the key advantages of cloud computing is its ability to provide access to software and resources from anywhere, at any time. This is particularly valuable for software engineering students who need access to powerful development tools and programming languages. With cloud computing, students can easily access these resources through a web browser, eliminating the need for local installations and ensuring compatibility across different devices and operating systems.

Additionally, cloud computing offers scalability and flexibility, allowing educational institutions to meet the changing needs of their students. As the demand for online learning continues to grow, cloud-based platforms enable educational institutions to scale their resources seamlessly, ensuring that students have uninterrupted access to learning materials and tools. Moreover, cloud computing enables collaborative projects and remote teamwork among software engineering students, facilitating real-time collaboration on code development and enhancing the overall learning experience.

However, despite the numerous benefits, cloud computing adoption in educational institutions is not without challenges. One of the primary concerns is data security and privacy. Educational institutions must ensure that student and faculty data are adequately protected, adhering to strict security protocols and compliance regulations. Furthermore, reliable internet connectivity is essential for seamless cloud computing adoption, and any disruptions can hinder the learning experience.

In conclusion, cloud computing adoption in educational institutions has transformed the way software engineering students access and utilize technology. By leveraging the scalability, flexibility, and accessibility of cloud computing, educational institutions can provide students with a more efficient and collaborative learning environment. However, it is crucial for institutions to address potential challenges such as data security and internet connectivity to fully realize the benefits of cloud computing in the educational setting.

Case Studies of Cloud Adoption in Schools and Universities

In recent years, cloud computing has revolutionized the way educational institutions manage their infrastructure. This subchapter aims to provide students in the field of software engineering with insightful case studies of cloud adoption in schools and universities. By examining real-life examples, students will gain a comprehensive understanding of the benefits and challenges associated with cloud computing in the education sector.

Case Study 1: XYZ University

XYZ University, renowned for its software engineering program, faced numerous challenges in managing its ever-growing infrastructure. The university's IT department implemented a cloud solution to address these issues. By migrating their applications and data to the cloud, the university experienced significant improvements in scalability, reliability, and cost-effectiveness. Students studying software engineering at XYZ University now have access to cutting-edge tools and resources that are easily accessible from anywhere, enabling seamless collaboration and enhancing their learning experience.

Case Study 2: ABC High School

ABC High School faced limitations in terms of hardware and software resources for its software engineering curriculum. To overcome these challenges, the school decided to adopt cloud-based solutions. By leveraging the cloud, the school was able to provide students with virtual development environments, allowing them to practice coding and work on projects without the need for expensive hardware or software installations. This cloud adoption not only reduced costs but also increased the school's ability to offer a comprehensive software engineering curriculum.

Case Study 3: DEF Technical Institute

DEF Technical Institute recognized the need to equip its students with the latest software engineering skills to prepare them for the job market. By adopting cloud computing, the institute was able to provide students with access to industry-leading software and tools, which otherwise would have been unaffordable. This cloud-based approach enabled students to gain hands-on experience with cutting-edge technologies, giving them a competitive edge in the software engineering field.

These case studies highlight the transformative impact of cloud adoption in educational institutions. By embracing cloud computing, schools and universities can overcome infrastructure challenges, enhance learning experiences, and provide students with the necessary tools to excel in software engineering. Whether it is improving accessibility, reducing costs, or fostering collaboration, the cloud has proven to be an invaluable asset for the education sector.

As students pursuing software engineering, understanding these case studies will empower you to recognize the potential of cloud computing in transforming infrastructure management. By staying informed about real-world examples, you will be well-equipped to navigate the evolving landscape of technology and leverage cloud solutions to drive innovation in your future careers.

Benefits and Challenges of Cloud Computing in Education

In recent years, cloud computing has revolutionized various industries, and the education sector is no exception. The adoption of cloud computing in education has brought about significant benefits, as well as a few challenges, particularly for students pursuing software engineering. This subchapter aims to explore the advantages and potential challenges that arise when integrating cloud computing into the field of education, specifically for students in software engineering.

One of the key benefits of cloud computing in education is the accessibility it provides. Students can access their educational resources, such as software tools, programming languages, and learning materials, from any device with an internet connection. This level of flexibility allows students to work on projects and assignments at their convenience, enhancing their productivity and time management skills. Additionally, cloud-based platforms often offer collaborative features, enabling students to collaborate seamlessly with their peers on group projects.

Another notable advantage of cloud computing in education is the cost-effectiveness it offers. Traditional software and hardware used in software engineering can be quite expensive for students, especially when starting their educational journey. Cloud computing eliminates the need for students to invest heavily in physical infrastructure, as they can utilize virtual environments and platforms provided by cloud service providers. This not only reduces the financial burden but also ensures that students have access to the latest software and tools without the need for constant upgrades.

However, incorporating cloud computing into education does come with its fair share of challenges. One such challenge is the dependency on internet connectivity. Since cloud computing relies heavily on internet connectivity, students may face difficulties accessing their resources or working on projects in areas with poor or unreliable internet connections. This challenge can be mitigated by utilizing offline capabilities or finding alternative internet sources, but it remains an obstacle that students must be prepared to tackle.

Additionally, security and privacy concerns can arise when using cloud-based platforms. Students must be aware of the potential risks associated with storing sensitive data on cloud servers and take appropriate precautions to protect their information. Understanding data encryption, access controls, and regularly updating passwords are essential practices to ensure the security of their work.

In conclusion, cloud computing offers numerous benefits for students in software engineering, including accessibility, cost-effectiveness, and collaborative capabilities. However, challenges such as internet connectivity and security concerns must be addressed to fully leverage the advantages of cloud computing in education. By understanding and navigating these challenges, students can harness the power of cloud computing to enhance their learning experience and prepare themselves for the future of infrastructure management in the software engineering field.

Infrastructure Management in Student Projects

As software engineering students, it is essential to understand the significance of infrastructure management in our projects. In this subchapter, we will explore the role of infrastructure management and how cloud computing can revolutionize the way we handle our projects.

Infrastructure management refers to the process of planning, deploying, and maintaining the underlying hardware and software components that support an application or system. It involves tasks such as server management, network configuration, storage allocation, and security measures. Effective infrastructure management ensures that our projects run smoothly, securely, and efficiently.

Cloud computing, with its vast array of services and resources, has transformed the way we approach infrastructure management. It offers scalable and on-demand access to computing resources, eliminating the need for physical infrastructure setup and maintenance. As students, utilizing cloud services enables us to focus more on developing and testing our software rather than worrying about infrastructure-related tasks.

One of the primary advantages of cloud computing in infrastructure management is cost savings. Traditional infrastructure setup requires significant upfront investments, whereas cloud services offer pay-as-you-go pricing models. This allows students to work within their budget constraints and allocate resources as needed, avoiding unnecessary expenses.

Furthermore, cloud computing provides flexibility and scalability. With a few clicks, we can easily scale up or down our infrastructure to accommodate changing project requirements. This is particularly beneficial when working on projects with varying workloads or when collaborating with team members who are located in different parts of the world.

Security is another crucial aspect of infrastructure management. Cloud service providers invest heavily in ensuring the security of their platforms, employing advanced encryption techniques, regular backups, and robust authentication mechanisms. By leveraging these services, we can focus on securing our applications rather than worrying about the security of our underlying infrastructure.

In conclusion, infrastructure management plays a vital role in software engineering projects. Cloud computing offers a revolutionary approach to infrastructure management, providing cost savings, flexibility, scalability, and enhanced security. As students, embracing cloud services allows us to focus on our core development tasks, ultimately leading to more efficient and successful project outcomes.

Collaborative Tools and Platforms for Student Projects

In today's fast-paced digital world, collaboration has become an essential aspect of any successful project. As students pursuing a degree in software engineering, it is crucial to understand and utilize the various collaborative tools and platforms available to enhance your project management skills. This subchapter aims to introduce you to some of the most effective tools and platforms that can revolutionize how you work on student projects, ensuring seamless collaboration and efficient teamwork.

One of the most popular collaborative tools among students is cloud-based project management software. These platforms, such as Trello, Asana, and Jira, provide a central hub for organizing tasks, assigning responsibilities, and tracking progress. With features like task assignment, real-time updates, and file sharing, these tools streamline communication and ensure everyone is on the same page. Additionally, these platforms offer integration with other tools, such as GitHub or Bitbucket, allowing for seamless code collaboration and version control.

Another essential collaborative tool for software engineering students is code collaboration platforms like GitLab and GitHub. These platforms enable multiple developers to work on the same codebase simultaneously, making it easier to spot errors, suggest improvements, and merge changes. By utilizing features such as pull requests and code reviews, students can learn from each other's coding styles and enhance the overall quality of their projects.

For real-time collaboration and communication, students can leverage platforms like Slack or Microsoft Teams. These messaging platforms offer channels dedicated to specific topics or project discussions, allowing for easy information sharing and quick problem-solving. With features like video calls, screen sharing, and file uploads, students can collaborate seamlessly even when physically apart.

In addition to these tools, it is essential to consider the power of collaborative document editing platforms like Google Docs or Microsoft Office 365. These platforms enable multiple users to work on the same document simultaneously, making it easier to gather inputs, make revisions, and maintain a centralized source of information. This is particularly useful when working on project documentation or reports, as it eliminates the hassle of merging different versions manually.

In conclusion, as software engineering students, embracing collaborative tools and platforms is essential for successful project management. By utilizing cloud-based project management software, code collaboration platforms, real-time communication tools, and collaborative document editing platforms, students can enhance their teamwork, streamline communication, and ultimately deliver high-quality projects. Embrace these tools and platforms, and witness how they transform your student projects into seamless collaborations that set you apart in the field of software engineering.

Data Storage and Backup Solutions for Students

In today's digital age, students in the field of software engineering are faced with the challenge of managing and safeguarding their valuable data. Whether it's assignments, projects, or personal documents, having a reliable storage and backup solution is essential to ensure the safety and accessibility of their digital assets. In this subchapter, we will explore some of the best data storage and backup solutions tailored specifically for students in the software engineering niche.

Cloud storage has emerged as one of the most popular and convenient solutions for students. Services like Google Drive, Dropbox, and Microsoft OneDrive offer free storage space and allow easy access to files from any device with an internet connection. These platforms provide seamless integration with popular productivity tools such as Google Docs and Microsoft Office, enabling collaborative work among team members. Additionally, cloud storage ensures data security with features like encryption and multi-factor authentication, giving students peace of mind knowing their files are protected.

Another option for data storage and backup is external hard drives or solid-state drives (SSDs). These portable devices provide ample storage capacity and allow students to keep a local copy of their files. They are particularly useful for situations where internet access is limited or when large files need to be transferred quickly. However, it's important to regularly back up the data from these devices to avoid potential loss or damage.

For students who prefer a more hands-on approach, setting up a personal network-attached storage (NAS) device can be a viable option. A NAS device acts as a private cloud server, allowing students to store and access their files directly from their home network. This solution provides complete control over data management and eliminates concerns about third-party access. However, it requires some technical knowledge to set up and maintain.

Lastly, utilizing version control systems like GitHub or Bitbucket can be an excellent choice for students in software engineering. These platforms not only offer storage for code repositories but also provide revision history, collaboration features, and the ability to roll back changes. Version control systems are essential tools for students working on software projects, enabling them to track and manage their code effectively.

In conclusion, students in the field of software engineering have various data storage and backup solutions to choose from. Cloud storage, external devices, personal NAS, and version control systems offer different benefits and cater to different needs. It is crucial for students to evaluate their requirements and select a solution that best fits their workflow and ensures the protection of their valuable data. By implementing a reliable data storage and backup strategy, students can focus on their academic pursuits with confidence and peace of mind.

Chapter 5: Security and Privacy in Cloud Computing

Cloud Security Fundamentals

As the world rapidly embraces cloud computing, it becomes crucial for students in the field of software engineering to understand the fundamentals of cloud security. With this knowledge, they can ensure the protection and privacy of data stored and transmitted in the cloud. This subchapter aims to provide an overview of the key principles and practices related to cloud security, equipping students with the necessary tools to design and develop secure cloud-based applications.

1.   Introduction   to   Cloud   Security: Cloud security refers to the set of policies, technologies, and controls implemented to protect cloud-based systems and data from unauthorized access, data breaches, and other cyber threats. Students will explore the importance of cloud security in maintaining the confidentiality, integrity, and availability of information stored in the cloud.

2.   Shared   Responsibility   Model: Understanding the shared responsibility model is crucial for students to grasp the division of security responsibilities between cloud service providers (CSPs) and cloud users. This section will explain the shared responsibility model, emphasizing the need for students to be proactive in securing their applications and data within the cloud.

3.   Threats   and   Vulnerabilities   in   the   Cloud: Students will learn about common threats and vulnerabilities associated with cloud computing, such as data breaches, unauthorized access, insider threats, and distributed denial-of-service (DDoS) attacks. This section will highlight the importance of continuously

monitoring and mitigating these risks through various security measures.

4. Security Controls and Technologies: Exploring the various security controls and technologies available in the cloud will enable students to design and implement robust security measures. Topics covered in this section may include encryption, identity and access management (IAM), network security, and data loss prevention.

5. Compliance and Legal Considerations: Compliance with industry regulations and legal requirements is essential when dealing with sensitive data in the cloud. Students will understand the importance of compliance frameworks and the legal considerations they must keep in mind when designing cloud-based applications.

6. Best Practices for Cloud Security: This section will provide students with a comprehensive set of best practices for ensuring cloud security. From secure coding practices to regular security assessments and incident response planning, students will learn how to integrate security into their cloud-based applications from the ground up.

In conclusion, mastering the fundamentals of cloud security is essential for students in the field of software engineering. By understanding the shared responsibility model, identifying threats and vulnerabilities, and implementing security controls and best practices, students will be equipped to develop secure and resilient cloud-based applications that meet the highest standards of data protection and privacy.

Authentication and Access Control in the Cloud

In today's digital era, cloud computing has emerged as a revolutionary technology, transforming the way businesses and individuals store, process, and access their data. As students studying software engineering, it is crucial to grasp the concepts of authentication and access control in the cloud, as they are fundamental to ensuring the security and integrity of cloud-based systems.

Authentication is the process of verifying the identity of a user or system before granting access to resources or data. In the cloud, authentication plays a vital role in protecting sensitive information from unauthorized access. Traditional methods of authentication, such as username and password, are still prevalent in the cloud environment. However, cloud service providers have introduced advanced authentication mechanisms, including multi-factor authentication (MFA) and biometric authentication, to enhance security.

MFA goes beyond the traditional username and password approach by requiring users to provide additional forms of identification, such as a fingerprint or a unique code generated on their mobile device. This adds an extra layer of security, making it significantly harder for unauthorized individuals to gain access to cloud resources. Biometric authentication, on the other hand, utilizes unique physical attributes, such as fingerprints or facial recognition, to confirm a user's identity. This method offers a higher level of security as biometric data is difficult to replicate.

Access control, on the other hand, involves managing and regulating user access to specific resources or data within a cloud environment. It ensures that users are granted appropriate permissions based on their roles and responsibilities. Cloud service providers offer various access control mechanisms, including role-based access control (RBAC) and attribute-based access control (ABAC).

RBAC allows system administrators to assign predefined roles to users, and each role has a set of permissions associated with it. This approach simplifies access management by eliminating the need to assign permissions individually for each user. ABAC, on the other hand, takes a more granular approach, considering attributes such as user attributes, resource attributes, and environmental attributes to determine access rights. This provides more flexibility and fine-grained control over access management.

As software engineering students, understanding the concepts of authentication and access control in the cloud is essential for designing and developing secure cloud-based applications. By implementing robust authentication mechanisms and employing effective access control policies, developers can ensure the confidentiality, integrity, and availability of data stored and processed in the cloud.

In conclusion, authentication and access control are critical components of cloud computing, ensuring the security and privacy of cloud-based systems. By utilizing advanced authentication methods and implementing appropriate access control mechanisms, software engineering students can contribute to the development of secure and reliable cloud-based applications. Keeping up with the latest trends and best practices in this domain will equip students with the necessary skills to succeed in their future careers in software engineering.

Data Encryption and Protection

In today's interconnected world, where data breaches and cyberattacks have become increasingly common, it is imperative for software engineering students to have a solid understanding of data encryption and protection. As they embark on their journey into the field of infrastructure management and cloud computing, it is crucial for them to recognize the significance of safeguarding sensitive information.

Data encryption serves as a powerful tool in protecting data from unauthorized access. It involves the conversion of plain text into an unintelligible form, known as ciphertext, using complex algorithms and keys. This process ensures that even if the data falls into the wrong hands, it remains unreadable and unusable. Encryption is widely utilized in various sectors, including finance, healthcare, and government, to secure sensitive information.

One of the fundamental encryption techniques used today is symmetric encryption. It involves the use of a single key, known as the secret key, for both encryption and decryption. This key must be kept confidential, as anyone who possesses it can access the encrypted data. On the other hand, asymmetric encryption employs a pair of keys – a public key for encryption and a private key for decryption. This method provides enhanced security as the private key remains solely with the data owner, while the public key can be freely distributed.

Furthermore, software engineering students must familiarize themselves with encryption algorithms, such as Advanced Encryption Standard (AES), RSA, and Triple DES. These algorithms differ in terms of their speed, level of security, and key sizes. While AES is known for its efficiency and strength, RSA is commonly used for secure data transmission. Triple DES, on the other hand, applies multiple encryption and decryption processes to enhance security.

In addition to encryption, protecting data also involves implementing robust security measures. This includes user authentication, access controls, and regular system updates. Students need to understand the importance of strong passwords, two-factor authentication, and the principle of least privilege to ensure that only authorized individuals can access sensitive data.

As future software engineers and infrastructure managers, it is crucial for students to prioritize data encryption and protection. By equipping themselves with the knowledge and skills necessary to secure digital assets, they will play a pivotal role in safeguarding sensitive information in the ever-evolving digital landscape.

Privacy Concerns in Cloud Computing

As technology continues to advance, cloud computing has emerged as a powerful tool for software engineering and infrastructure management. However, it also raises significant privacy concerns that students in the field of software engineering need to be aware of. In this subchapter, we will explore these concerns and their implications.

One of the main privacy concerns in cloud computing is data security. When utilizing cloud services, individuals and organizations store their data on remote servers maintained by cloud service providers. While these providers generally have robust security measures in place, there is always a risk of unauthorized access or data breaches. Students need to understand the importance of encryption, strong access controls, and regular security audits to ensure data privacy in the cloud.

Another concern is data ownership and control. When data is stored in the cloud, it becomes subject to the terms and conditions set by the service provider. Students must be aware of these terms and understand who has access to their data, how it can be used, and if it can be shared with third parties. It is crucial to read and comprehend the service level agreements (SLAs) and privacy policies of cloud providers to make informed decisions about data storage and management.

Furthermore, the issue of data location and jurisdiction arises in cloud computing. Cloud service providers may have servers located in different countries or regions, which have varying data protection laws. Students should consider the legal implications of storing data in different jurisdictions and be cognizant of potential conflicts between local regulations and international data transfer policies.

Additionally, students must recognize the potential risks associated with vendor lock-in. When organizations heavily rely on a specific cloud provider's infrastructure, it becomes challenging to switch to another provider or bring the data back in-house. This lack of interoperability can limit flexibility and hinder future technological advancements. Understanding the potential consequences of vendor lock-in can help students make informed decisions when choosing cloud service providers.

In conclusion, while cloud computing offers numerous benefits for software engineering and infrastructure management, it also raises significant privacy concerns. Students in the field need to be well-versed in data security, ownership, jurisdiction, and vendor lock-in to navigate the cloud environment safely and responsibly. By understanding the potential risks and implementing necessary safeguards, students can utilize cloud computing effectively while protecting privacy and data integrity.

Compliance with Data Protection Regulations

In today's digital age, the importance of data protection cannot be overstated. As students venturing into the field of software engineering, it is crucial to understand and comply with data protection regulations. This subchapter aims to shed light on the significance of data protection, the existing regulations, and how they impact the field of software engineering.

Data protection regulations are designed to safeguard individuals' personal information and ensure that organizations handle it responsibly. The most prominent regulation in this area is the General Data Protection Regulation (GDPR), which was introduced by the European Union in 2018. GDPR sets out strict guidelines for the collection, storage, and processing of personal data. As software engineers, it is essential to be aware of these regulations and incorporate them into our work.

Complying with data protection regulations involves several key aspects. Firstly, it is vital to understand the types of data that fall under the purview of these regulations. Personal data includes any information that can directly or indirectly identify an individual, such as names, addresses, or even IP addresses. As software engineers, we must be mindful of the data we handle and ensure its protection.

Another crucial aspect is obtaining informed consent from individuals before collecting their personal data. This means explaining how their data will be used, stored, and processed, and giving them the option to provide or withhold consent. It is our responsibility as software engineers to design systems that facilitate this consent process and ensure transparency.

Furthermore, data protection regulations require implementing appropriate security measures to safeguard personal data against unauthorized access, loss, or breach. As software engineers, we must utilize encryption, access controls, and other security practices to protect the data we handle.

Non-compliance with data protection regulations can have severe consequences, including hefty fines and damage to an organization's reputation. Therefore, it is essential for software engineers to stay updated with the latest developments in data protection and ensure compliance in their work.

In conclusion, compliance with data protection regulations is of utmost importance for software engineers. Understanding the regulations, obtaining informed consent, implementing robust security measures, and staying up-to-date with the evolving landscape of data protection are all crucial aspects of our work. By prioritizing data protection, we not only fulfill our legal obligations but also contribute to building a more secure and trustworthy digital ecosystem.

Data Ownership and Control in the Cloud

In today's digital age, where data is the new currency, understanding the concepts of data ownership and control in the cloud is essential for students pursuing a career in software engineering. Cloud computing has revolutionized the way businesses store and manage their data, offering unparalleled convenience and scalability. However, it also raises concerns about who owns the data and how much control individuals and organizations have over it.

Data ownership refers to the legal rights and control that individuals or organizations have over the data they generate or store in the cloud. In a traditional on-premises infrastructure, data ownership is relatively straightforward, as the data resides within the organization's physical boundaries. However, in the cloud, data is stored and processed by third-party service providers, introducing complexities in determining ownership.

When using cloud services, it is crucial to carefully review the terms and conditions of the service provider to understand the ownership rights granted to users. Some providers may claim ownership over the data stored on their servers, while others may explicitly state that users retain full ownership. Students must be aware of these nuances and ensure that they select cloud providers that align with their data ownership preferences.

Control over data in the cloud refers to the ability to access, manage, and protect the data stored in cloud services. While cloud providers offer robust security measures, students must take an active role in understanding and implementing additional security controls to safeguard their data. This includes implementing strong access controls, encryption, and regular data backups.

Additionally, students should be aware of the risks associated with third-party data breaches or unauthorized access. Cloud providers typically have stringent security protocols in place, but it is vital for students to be proactive in monitoring their data and promptly reporting any suspicious activities to the provider.

Furthermore, understanding data portability is crucial when discussing data ownership and control in the cloud. Students should be familiar with the process of migrating their data from one cloud provider to another, as well as the potential challenges and limitations involved. This knowledge will empower them to make informed decisions about their data and avoid vendor lock-in.

In conclusion, data ownership and control in the cloud are critical considerations for students pursuing a career in software engineering. By understanding the legal rights and responsibilities associated with data ownership, implementing robust security measures, and being knowledgeable about data portability, students can confidently navigate the complexities of cloud computing and make informed decisions to protect their valuable data.

Chapter 6: Future Trends and Emerging Technologies in Cloud Computing

Edge Computing and its Implications for Infrastructure Management

In recent years, the field of infrastructure management has witnessed a significant paradigm shift with the advent of edge computing. As students studying software engineering, it is crucial to understand the implications of this cutting-edge technology on infrastructure management. This subchapter aims to provide you with an in-depth exploration of edge computing and its implications for infrastructure management.

Edge computing refers to the decentralized processing of data at the edge of a network, closer to the source where it is generated. Unlike traditional cloud computing, where data is sent to a centralized data center for processing, edge computing brings the computing power closer to the devices and sensors generating the data. This proximity enables faster data processing, reduced latency, and enhanced efficiency.

One of the key implications of edge computing for infrastructure management is the ability to handle massive volumes of real-time data. With the proliferation of Internet of Things (IoT) devices and sensors, the amount of data generated has grown exponentially. Edge computing allows for the processing of this data at the edge, reducing the strain on the network and minimizing latency. This enables faster decision-making and real-time responses, which is crucial in sectors such as autonomous vehicles, healthcare, and manufacturing.

Moreover, edge computing reduces the dependency on a centralized infrastructure, making it more robust and resilient. By distributing the computing power across multiple edge devices, the risk of a single point of failure is significantly reduced. This distributed architecture ensures continuous operations even in the event of network outages or disruptions. As software engineers, it is essential to design and develop applications that can leverage this distributed infrastructure effectively.

Furthermore, edge computing enables the development of intelligent and autonomous systems. By processing data at the edge, devices can make localized decisions and take immediate actions without relying on a cloud-based infrastructure. This has significant implications for applications such as smart cities, where real-time responses and autonomous decision-making are crucial for efficient resource management.

In conclusion, edge computing is revolutionizing the field of infrastructure management. As software engineering students, understanding its implications is vital for designing and developing applications that can leverage the benefits of this technology. Edge computing enables the handling of massive volumes of real-time data, reduces dependency on a centralized infrastructure, and empowers the development of intelligent and autonomous systems. Embracing edge computing will undoubtedly shape the future of infrastructure management in the era of IoT and smart technologies.

Artificial Intelligence and Machine Learning in Cloud Computing

In recent years, the integration of Artificial Intelligence (AI) and Machine Learning (ML) with cloud computing has revolutionized the field of software engineering. This subchapter aims to explore the exciting possibilities and applications that arise from combining these cutting-edge technologies.

Cloud computing provides a scalable and flexible infrastructure for storing and processing vast amounts of data. By leveraging the power of the cloud, AI and ML algorithms can be deployed and executed efficiently, enabling faster and more accurate analyses. The cloud's ability to provide on-demand resources allows software engineers to scale their AI and ML systems seamlessly, accommodating the ever-growing data requirements.

One of the significant benefits of utilizing AI and ML in the cloud is the ability to automate complex tasks and decision-making processes. Students studying software engineering can leverage these technologies to develop intelligent systems that can learn from data, adapt to changing conditions, and make informed decisions. For instance, AI-driven chatbots can be integrated into cloud-based applications to provide personalized customer support, enhancing user experience.

Moreover, cloud-based AI and ML can greatly benefit software engineers in developing predictive analytics solutions. By analyzing vast amounts of historical data stored in the cloud, these technologies can identify patterns and correlations that may not be apparent to human analysts. Students can develop predictive models that assist in making critical business decisions, such as demand forecasting, risk assessment, or fraud detection.

Another exciting application of AI and ML in cloud computing is the development of intelligent recommendation systems. By leveraging user data stored in the cloud, software engineers can create personalized recommendations for products, services, or content. For example, streaming platforms can suggest movies or songs based on a user's preferences and previous viewing history, leading to a more engaging and tailored user experience.

Furthermore, the integration of AI and ML with cloud computing enables the development of autonomous systems. Students can explore the realm of self-driving cars, drones, or robots that utilize cloud-based AI algorithms to navigate, perceive the environment, and make real-time decisions. This fusion of technologies presents exciting opportunities for software engineers to pioneer advancements in automation and robotics.

In conclusion, the integration of Artificial Intelligence and Machine Learning with cloud computing brings forth a myriad of possibilities for students studying software engineering. The ability to leverage the cloud's scalability and flexibility, combined with the power of AI and ML algorithms, allows for the development of intelligent systems, predictive analytics solutions, recommendation systems, and autonomous technologies. By understanding and mastering these technologies, students can position themselves at the forefront of innovation in the future of infrastructure management.

Blockchain Technology in Cloud Computing

Blockchain technology has emerged as a revolutionary innovation that has the potential to transform various industries, including cloud computing. In this subchapter, we will explore the integration of blockchain technology in cloud computing and its implications for software engineering students.

Cloud computing has revolutionized the way businesses, organizations, and individuals access and manage their data and applications. It provides a scalable and flexible infrastructure that allows users to access computing resources on-demand. However, traditional cloud computing systems are centralized, which raises concerns about data security, privacy, and trust.

Blockchain technology, on the other hand, offers a decentralized approach to data management and transaction verification. It is a distributed ledger that records transactions across multiple computers or nodes. Each transaction, or block, is encrypted and linked to the previous block, forming a chain of blocks. This decentralized and immutable nature of blockchain technology brings several advantages to cloud computing.

One of the key benefits of integrating blockchain technology in cloud computing is enhanced security. Traditional cloud computing systems are vulnerable to data breaches and cyber-attacks due to their centralized nature. By decentralizing data storage and adopting blockchain technology, the risk of data manipulation or unauthorized access is significantly reduced. Blockchain provides a tamper-proof and transparent record of all transactions, ensuring data integrity and enhancing security for software engineering students working with sensitive data.

Another advantage of blockchain technology in cloud computing is increased trust and transparency. As blockchain technology enables a distributed network, it eliminates the need for intermediaries and enables direct peer-to-peer interactions. This transparency allows software engineering students to verify and validate the authenticity of data and applications, ensuring that they are working with reliable and trustworthy resources.

Moreover, blockchain technology in cloud computing also offers improved efficiency and cost-effectiveness. By eliminating intermediaries and enabling direct transactions, blockchain reduces the complexity and costs associated with traditional cloud computing systems. It also enables more efficient resource allocation and utilization, optimizing the overall performance of cloud computing infrastructure.

In conclusion, the integration of blockchain technology in cloud computing holds great promise for software engineering students. It offers enhanced security, increased trust and transparency, and improved efficiency and cost-effectiveness. As the demand for secure and reliable cloud computing solutions continues to rise, understanding blockchain technology becomes crucial for students entering the field of software engineering. By embracing blockchain technology, students can contribute to the development of innovative and secure cloud computing solutions that will shape the future of infrastructure management.

Chapter 7: Best Practices for Students in Cloud Computing and Infrastructure Management

Selecting the Right Cloud Service Provider for Student Needs

In today's digital era, cloud computing has revolutionized the way we store and access data. For students pursuing a career in software engineering, having a reliable and efficient cloud service provider is crucial. With numerous options available in the market, it can be overwhelming to choose the right one that caters to your specific needs. This subchapter aims to guide students in selecting the ideal cloud service provider for their software engineering endeavors.

Before delving into the selection process, it is essential to understand the benefits of cloud computing for students. Cloud services offer the ability to store and access data from any device with an internet connection, providing seamless collaboration and flexibility. Additionally, the cloud offers scalable resources, allowing students to expand their projects without worrying about hardware limitations.

The first step in selecting a cloud service provider is to assess your requirements. Consider factors such as storage capacity, computing power, and security features. As a software engineering student, you may require a provider that supports multiple programming languages, offers development environments, or provides access to specialized tools.

Security should be a top priority when selecting a cloud service provider. Look for providers that offer robust encryption, secure data centers, and compliance with industry standards such as GDPR. Additionally, check if the provider offers backup and disaster recovery options to ensure the safety of your data.

Cost is another significant factor to consider. As a student, you may have budget constraints, so it's crucial to find a provider that offers a pricing model that aligns with your needs. Some providers offer free tiers for limited usage, while others offer discounted plans for students.

Furthermore, consider the provider's reliability and uptime. Downtime can significantly impact your productivity, so ensure the provider has a strong track record of uptime and provides reliable customer support.

Lastly, take into account the provider's ecosystem and integration capabilities. A provider that integrates well with popular software development tools and platforms can streamline your workflow and enhance collaboration with peers.

In conclusion, selecting the right cloud service provider is vital for software engineering students. By considering factors such as requirements, security, cost, reliability, and integration capabilities, students can make an informed decision. Remember to thoroughly research and compare different providers before committing to one. Choosing the right cloud service provider will not only enhance your software engineering projects but also prepare you for the future of infrastructure management.

Ensuring Data Security and Privacy in the Cloud

In today's rapidly evolving technological landscape, cloud computing has emerged as a powerful tool for managing infrastructure. As students pursuing a career in software engineering, it is crucial to understand the importance of data security and privacy in the context of cloud computing. This subchapter will delve into the various measures and best practices that can be employed to safeguard sensitive information stored in the cloud.

The cloud offers numerous benefits, such as scalability, cost-efficiency, and easy access to resources. However, it also introduces unique challenges, particularly concerning the security and privacy of data. As software engineers, you must be equipped with the knowledge and skills to address these challenges effectively.

One of the fundamental steps in ensuring data security is employing strong authentication and access control mechanisms. This involves implementing robust password policies, multi-factor authentication, and role-based access control to restrict unauthorized access to sensitive data. Additionally, encryption techniques should be used to protect data both in transit and at rest, mitigating the risk of unauthorized interception or data breaches.

Another crucial aspect is regular data backups and disaster recovery planning. Cloud service providers often offer automated backup solutions, but it is essential to understand the frequency and reliability of these backups. Furthermore, students should be familiar with disaster recovery strategies to ensure the availability and integrity of data in case of system failures or natural disasters.

Compliance with industry standards and regulations is equally paramount. Familiarize yourselves with data protection laws, such as the General Data Protection Regulation (GDPR), and ensure that any cloud service provider you choose adheres to these regulations. Being aware of these legal obligations will not only protect the privacy of user data but also safeguard against potential legal repercussions.

Finally, continuous monitoring and auditing of cloud resources are vital to identify and address any vulnerabilities or suspicious activities promptly. By implementing intrusion detection systems, log analysis tools, and routine security audits, software engineers can proactively detect and mitigate potential security risks.

In conclusion, as students in the field of software engineering, understanding data security and privacy in the cloud is of utmost importance. By implementing strong authentication measures, encryption techniques, disaster recovery plans, compliance with regulations, and continuous monitoring, you can ensure the safety and integrity of data stored in the cloud. Embracing these best practices will not only enhance your professional capabilities but also contribute to the overall trust and reliability of cloud computing systems.

Managing Cloud Costs and Usage

As students pursuing a career in software engineering, it is crucial to understand the importance of managing cloud costs and usage. Cloud computing has revolutionized the way businesses operate and has become an integral part of modern infrastructure management. However, without proper management and monitoring, cloud costs can quickly skyrocket, impacting the overall efficiency and profitability of organizations. Therefore, it is essential for students to grasp the strategies and best practices for managing cloud costs and usage effectively.

One fundamental aspect of managing cloud costs is optimization. Cloud providers offer a wide range of services, each with its pricing models. By analyzing the requirements of a particular project, students can select the most cost-effective services that meet the desired outcome. This optimization process involves understanding the pricing structures, considering the storage and compute needs, and identifying any potential cost-saving opportunities. By doing so, students can ensure that their cloud usage aligns with the budgetary constraints without compromising the project's objectives.

Furthermore, monitoring and analyzing cloud usage are critical for cost management. Cloud providers offer various tools and dashboards that allow users to monitor resource utilization, identify any underutilized or idle resources, and make informed decisions to optimize costs. Students should become proficient in leveraging these monitoring tools to track their cloud usage patterns, identify any anomalies, and make necessary adjustments to avoid unnecessary expenses.

Another essential aspect of cost management is the implementation of automation and scalability. By automating resource provisioning and deprovisioning, students can ensure that resources are allocated efficiently and only when required. This approach eliminates the risk of overspending on unnecessary resources and enables quick scalability when the demand increases. Understanding cloud orchestration tools and concepts such as auto-scaling will empower students to design and implement cost-efficient cloud solutions.

In addition to optimization, monitoring, and automation, students should also be aware of various cost management techniques, such as reserved instances, spot instances, and cost allocation tags. These techniques allow for further cost savings by leveraging discounted pricing options, bidding on spare cloud capacity, and allocating costs accurately across different projects or departments.

In conclusion, managing cloud costs and usage is a crucial skill for students specializing in software engineering. By focusing on optimization, monitoring, and automation, students can ensure that cloud resources are utilized efficiently and costs are kept under control. Familiarity with cost management techniques and tools will empower students to make informed decisions and contribute to the efficient and cost-effective utilization of cloud computing resources in their future careers.

Building Skills and Knowledge in Cloud Computing and Infrastructure Management

In today's digital era, cloud computing has emerged as a groundbreaking technology that has revolutionized the way businesses operate and individuals access information. As students pursuing a career in software engineering, it is imperative to have a deep understanding of cloud computing and infrastructure management to stay ahead in the competitive job market. This subchapter aims to provide you with valuable insights into building skills and knowledge in this rapidly evolving field.

Cloud computing refers to the delivery of computing services, including storage, servers, databases, networking, and software, over the internet. It offers immense scalability, flexibility, and cost-effectiveness, making it an indispensable tool for businesses of all sizes. By acquiring expertise in cloud computing, you will possess the ability to design, develop, and maintain cloud-based applications and infrastructures, a skillset highly sought after by employers.

To embark on your journey towards mastering cloud computing and infrastructure management, it is essential to start with a strong foundation in the underlying technologies. Familiarize yourself with concepts such as virtualization, networking, and storage systems, as these form the building blocks of cloud computing. Gain hands-on experience by setting up virtual machines, configuring networks, and managing storage systems on popular cloud platforms like Amazon Web Services (AWS), Microsoft Azure, or Google Cloud Platform (GCP).

Furthermore, it is crucial to stay updated with the latest trends and advancements in cloud computing. Attend webinars, conferences, and workshops to expand your knowledge and network with industry professionals. Engage in online communities and forums to exchange ideas, ask questions, and learn from experienced practitioners.

Acquiring relevant certifications can significantly enhance your employability in the field of cloud computing. Certifications such as AWS Certified Solutions Architect, Microsoft Certified: Azure Administrator, or Google Cloud Certified - Associate Cloud Engineer validate your skills and demonstrate your commitment to continuous learning.

Lastly, don't underestimate the importance of practical experience. Seek internships or part-time jobs in organizations that leverage cloud computing technologies. Apply your theoretical knowledge to real-world scenarios, and learn from experienced professionals who can provide valuable mentorship.

In conclusion, the future of infrastructure management lies in cloud computing. As students pursuing a career in software engineering, building skills and knowledge in this field is paramount. By understanding the underlying technologies, staying updated with the latest trends, obtaining relevant certifications, and gaining practical experience, you will position yourself as a valuable asset in the job market. Embrace the opportunities offered by cloud computing, and unlock a world of possibilities for your future career.

Chapter 8: Case Studies and Real-World Examples

Successful Implementation of Cloud Computing in Student Projects

In today's digital world, cloud computing has revolutionized the way we store, access, and process data. This innovative technology has not only transformed the way businesses operate but has also found its way into various educational fields, including software engineering. The implementation of cloud computing in student projects has proven to be immensely beneficial, offering an array of advantages that contribute to the success of these endeavors.

One of the primary benefits of utilizing cloud computing in student projects is the flexibility it provides. Unlike traditional methods that require local infrastructure and hardware, cloud computing allows students to access resources and tools from anywhere, at any time. This flexibility ensures that students can work on their projects seamlessly, whether they are on campus, at home, or even on the go. Furthermore, cloud computing enables collaboration among team members, regardless of their physical location, fostering teamwork and enhancing project outcomes.

Another significant advantage of implementing cloud computing in student projects is the scalability it offers. With cloud-based platforms, students can easily scale up or down their resources based on project requirements. This eliminates the need for extensive hardware upgrades, making it cost-effective and time-efficient. Additionally, the scalability of cloud computing allows students to experiment and explore new technologies without being limited by their local infrastructure, thus promoting innovation and creativity.

Security is a paramount concern when it comes to storing and processing sensitive data. Cloud computing provides robust security measures that ensure the safety of student projects. Cloud service providers employ advanced encryption techniques, access controls, and data backup mechanisms to protect the integrity and confidentiality of student data. By utilizing cloud computing, students can focus on their projects without worrying about data breaches or loss, thereby enhancing their productivity and peace of mind.

Furthermore, implementing cloud computing in student projects allows for real-time monitoring and analytics. Cloud-based platforms provide students with tools to monitor the performance and usage of their applications, enabling them to make data-driven decisions and optimize their projects accordingly. This invaluable feedback loop enhances the overall quality and efficiency of student projects, ensuring they meet the desired objectives.

In conclusion, the successful implementation of cloud computing in student projects has become a game-changer in the field of software engineering. The flexibility, scalability, security, and real-time monitoring offered by cloud computing significantly contribute to the success and effectiveness of student endeavors. By embracing cloud computing, students can maximize their potential, unleash their creativity, and shape the future of infrastructure management in the digital era.

Cloud Infrastructure Management in Educational Institutions

In recent years, cloud computing has emerged as a game-changer in the field of technology, revolutionizing the way organizations manage their infrastructure. Educational institutions, including universities and colleges, are no exception to this transformative trend. Cloud infrastructure management in educational institutions has become an essential aspect of modern-day learning environments. This subchapter aims to explore the significance of cloud computing for students pursuing software engineering.

Cloud infrastructure management refers to the administration and oversight of the various components of a cloud computing infrastructure that supports the educational institution's technological needs. This includes the management of servers, storage, networking, and virtualization, among other things. By utilizing cloud infrastructure management, educational institutions can enhance their software engineering programs and provide students with a cutting-edge learning experience.

One of the key advantages of cloud infrastructure management for students in the field of software engineering is the accessibility it offers. Through the cloud, students can access their coursework, development environments, and resources from any device with an internet connection. This flexibility allows for collaborative work, remote learning, and the ability to work on projects at any time, enhancing productivity and efficiency.

Furthermore, cloud infrastructure management enables educational institutions to offer a wide range of software tools and platforms to students. With cloud-based development environments, students can experiment with different programming languages, frameworks, and tools without the need for complex installations on their personal devices. This not only saves time but also provides an opportunity to explore new technologies and stay up-to-date with the latest industry trends.

Another significant benefit of cloud infrastructure management is the scalability it offers. Educational institutions can easily scale up or down their computing resources based on the needs of their software engineering programs. This ensures that students have access to powerful computing capabilities when working on resource-intensive tasks, such as running complex algorithms or simulations.

Moreover, cloud infrastructure management enhances data security and backup for students. Educational institutions can implement robust security measures and backup strategies to protect students' projects, assignments, and sensitive information. This eliminates the risk of data loss or unauthorized access, providing students with peace of mind and allowing them to focus solely on their learning.

In conclusion, cloud infrastructure management has revolutionized the way educational institutions manage their technological infrastructure, particularly in the field of software engineering. Through increased accessibility, a wide range of software tools, scalability, and enhanced data security, students can benefit greatly from the cloud. The future of infrastructure management in educational institutions lies in cloud computing, and students pursuing software engineering should embrace these advancements to stay ahead in this rapidly evolving field.

Cloud Computing Innovations for Students

Cloud computing has revolutionized the way software engineering students work and collaborate on projects. With its advanced capabilities and numerous benefits, cloud computing has become an indispensable tool for students in the field of software engineering. This subchapter will delve into the various innovations that cloud computing offers to students, enabling them to excel in their studies and future careers.

One of the key advantages of cloud computing for students is its ability to provide access to powerful computing resources. Traditionally, students relied on their personal computers or university resources, which often had limited processing power. However, with cloud computing, students can leverage the extensive computing capabilities of the cloud to run resource-intensive applications and simulations without the need for expensive hardware upgrades. This allows students to work on complex projects and experiment with cutting-edge technologies.

Moreover, cloud computing facilitates seamless collaboration among students. Through cloud-based collaboration tools, software engineering students can work together on projects, share code, and provide real-time feedback. This eliminates the need for physical meetings and simplifies the process of working in a team, even if the members are geographically dispersed. Cloud-based version control systems also enable students to track changes in their code, ensuring seamless integration and reducing the risk of conflicts.

Another innovation that cloud computing brings to students is the ability to access a wide range of software tools and development environments. Cloud-based Integrated Development Environments

(IDEs) provide students with a feature-rich coding environment that can be accessed from anywhere with an internet connection. This eliminates the need for installing and maintaining software packages on personal computers, making it easier for students to get started with coding and reducing compatibility issues.

Additionally, cloud computing offers cost savings for students. Instead of purchasing expensive software licenses or investing in hardware, students can opt for cloud-based solutions that are often available at a fraction of the cost. This allows students to explore and experiment with different software and tools without breaking the bank.

In conclusion, cloud computing innovations have transformed the landscape of software engineering education. Through access to powerful computing resources, seamless collaboration tools, a wide range of software tools, and cost savings, students can enhance their learning experience and prepare themselves for a successful career in software engineering. Embracing cloud computing is essential for students in this field, as it equips them with the necessary skills and knowledge to thrive in a rapidly evolving digital world.

Chapter 9: Conclusion and Future Outlook

Recap of Key Concepts and Takeaways

In this subchapter, we will provide a concise recap of the key concepts and takeaways discussed throughout the book "The Future of Infrastructure Management: Exploring Cloud Computing for Students." This recap is specifically tailored to students in the niche of software engineering, highlighting the most important points you should remember.

1. Cloud Computing Basics:
- Understand the fundamental concepts of cloud computing, including virtualization, scalability, and on-demand resource allocation.
- Recognize the different cloud service models: Infrastructure as a Service (IaaS), Platform as a Service (PaaS), and Software as a Service (SaaS).
- Comprehend the benefits of cloud computing, such as cost efficiency, flexibility, and global accessibility.

2. Infrastructure Management:
- Learn the importance of efficient infrastructure management in software engineering projects.
- Explore the challenges faced by traditional infrastructure management approaches and how cloud computing addresses those challenges.
- Understand the role of cloud service providers in managing infrastructure resources, ensuring reliability, security, and maintenance.

3. Cloud Deployment Models:
- Differentiate between public, private, hybrid, and community cloud

deployment models.
- Evaluate the advantages and limitations of each cloud deployment model based on specific software engineering requirements.
- Consider the factors influencing the selection of an appropriate deployment model, including cost, control, and compliance.

4. Security and Privacy Considerations:
- Recognize the potential security risks associated with cloud computing, such as data breaches and unauthorized access.
- Understand the strategies and best practices to ensure data security and privacy in the cloud environment.
- Familiarize yourself with compliance regulations, such as GDPR and HIPAA, and their impact on cloud-based software engineering projects.

5. Emerging Trends and Future Directions:
- Explore the latest advancements and trends in cloud computing, such as serverless computing, edge computing, and containerization.
- Understand the potential impact of these emerging technologies on software engineering practices and infrastructure management.
- Stay updated with the current research and developments in the field to remain competitive in the ever-evolving world of cloud computing.

By reviewing these key concepts and takeaways, you have gained a solid understanding of cloud computing and its implications for software engineering. Remember to continuously update your knowledge and skills as the field evolves, as staying ahead of the curve is crucial in this rapidly changing industry. Good luck on your cloud computing journey!

The Future of Infrastructure Management in Cloud Computing

Cloud computing has revolutionized the field of software engineering, and its impact on infrastructure management cannot be overstated. As students pursuing a career in software engineering, it is crucial to understand the future of infrastructure management in the context of cloud computing. This subchapter aims to provide you with insights into the exciting developments and opportunities that lie ahead.

One of the key aspects of the future of infrastructure management in cloud computing is the shift towards automation. Manual infrastructure management processes are being increasingly replaced by automated tools and frameworks. This shift not only improves efficiency but also reduces human error and operational costs. As a student, it is imperative to develop skills in automation tools and learn about the latest advancements in this area.

Another significant trend is the rise of containerization and microservices architecture. Containers enable the packaging of applications and their dependencies into portable units, making them easier to deploy and manage in a cloud environment. Microservices architecture, on the other hand, allows applications to be broken down into smaller, loosely coupled services, which can be independently developed, deployed, and scaled. Understanding containerization and microservices architecture is vital for future software engineers, as they will play a critical role in infrastructure management.

Security is another crucial aspect of infrastructure management in cloud computing. As more organizations move their applications and data to the cloud, ensuring the security and privacy of their infrastructure becomes paramount. Students must acquire knowledge of various security measures and best practices to protect sensitive information in a cloud environment.

The future also holds immense potential for machine learning and artificial intelligence in infrastructure management. These technologies can analyze vast amounts of data to identify patterns, optimize resource allocation, and predict potential issues. As aspiring software engineers, gaining expertise in machine learning and artificial intelligence will give you a competitive edge in the job market.

Lastly, the future of infrastructure management in cloud computing will witness the increased adoption of hybrid and multi-cloud environments. Organizations are increasingly leveraging multiple cloud providers and combining private and public clouds to meet their specific requirements. Understanding how to manage and integrate different cloud platforms will be essential for software engineers.

In conclusion, the future of infrastructure management in cloud computing is filled with exciting possibilities. Automation, containerization, security, machine learning, and hybrid cloud environments are the key trends that students in software engineering should focus on. By staying abreast of these developments, you will be well-prepared to shape the future of infrastructure management in the cloud.

Recommendations for Students and Educational Institutions

In today's rapidly evolving technological landscape, it is crucial for students pursuing a career in software engineering to stay abreast of the latest developments in infrastructure management. As the world increasingly relies on cloud computing, it is imperative for students and educational institutions to adapt and integrate this technology into their academic programs. This subchapter aims to provide recommendations for students and educational institutions to optimize their learning and teaching experiences in the field of software engineering.

First and foremost, students should familiarize themselves with the fundamentals of cloud computing. Understanding the basic concepts, such as virtualization, scalability, and elasticity, will lay a strong foundation for their future endeavors. They should seek out online resources, attend webinars, and participate in workshops to enhance their understanding of cloud technologies.

To gain hands-on experience, students should explore opportunities to work on real-world cloud projects. Collaborating with industry professionals or participating in internships at cloud service providers will provide invaluable exposure to the practical aspects of infrastructure management. Additionally, students can contribute to open-source projects related to cloud computing, which will not only enhance their skills but also allow them to showcase their abilities to potential employers.

Educational institutions, on the other hand, should incorporate cloud computing courses and workshops into their software engineering curricula. By doing so, they can ensure that students are equipped with the necessary knowledge and skills to thrive in the digital age.

Moreover, institutions should establish partnerships with cloud service providers to offer internships, guest lectures, and mentorship programs, creating a bridge between academia and industry.

To foster a collaborative learning environment, educational institutions should encourage students to form study groups or join cloud computing clubs. These platforms will enable students to share their knowledge, exchange ideas, and solve problems collectively. Additionally, institutions should organize hackathons or competitions centered around cloud computing to stimulate innovation and creativity among students.

Lastly, students and educational institutions should stay updated with the latest advancements in cloud computing. Following industry blogs, subscribing to newsletters, and attending conferences will help both parties stay at the forefront of this rapidly evolving field.

In conclusion, the adoption of cloud computing in software engineering has become inevitable. Students must embrace this technology by acquiring the necessary skills and practical experience, while educational institutions should adapt their curricula to integrate cloud computing courses. By following these recommendations, students and educational institutions can ensure a successful transition into the future of infrastructure management.